Kids' Guide to Gardening Like a Pro

Simple gardening curriculum for 5th grade through 8th grade

Gardening can be an enriching educational experience for students in 5th through 8th grade. Here's a simple gardening curriculum that covers various aspects of gardening and plant life. It is specifically designed to engage and educate students in these grade levels.

Week 1: Introduction to Gardening

Objectives

- Discuss the importance of gardening and its benefits.
- Explore different types of gardens (vegetable, herb, flower) and their purposes.
- Introduction to basic gardening tools and their uses.

Gardening is a wonderful activity that involves growing and caring for plants. It offers many benefits, such as promoting health, providing fresh food, and beautifying our surroundings.

In gardening, we can create different types of gardens, like vegetable gardens for growing edible plants, herb gardens for culinary and medicinal herbs, and flower gardens for visual appeal.

Basic gardening tools, like a hand trowel, pruning shears, and a watering can, help us in planting, maintaining, and nurturing our plants. So, let's get started and experience the joys of gardening!

Week 2: Understanding Plants

Objectives:

- Learn about the parts of a plant (roots, stems, leaves, flowers, fruits).
- Discuss the functions of each plant part.
- Conduct a hands-on activity to examine and identify different plant parts.

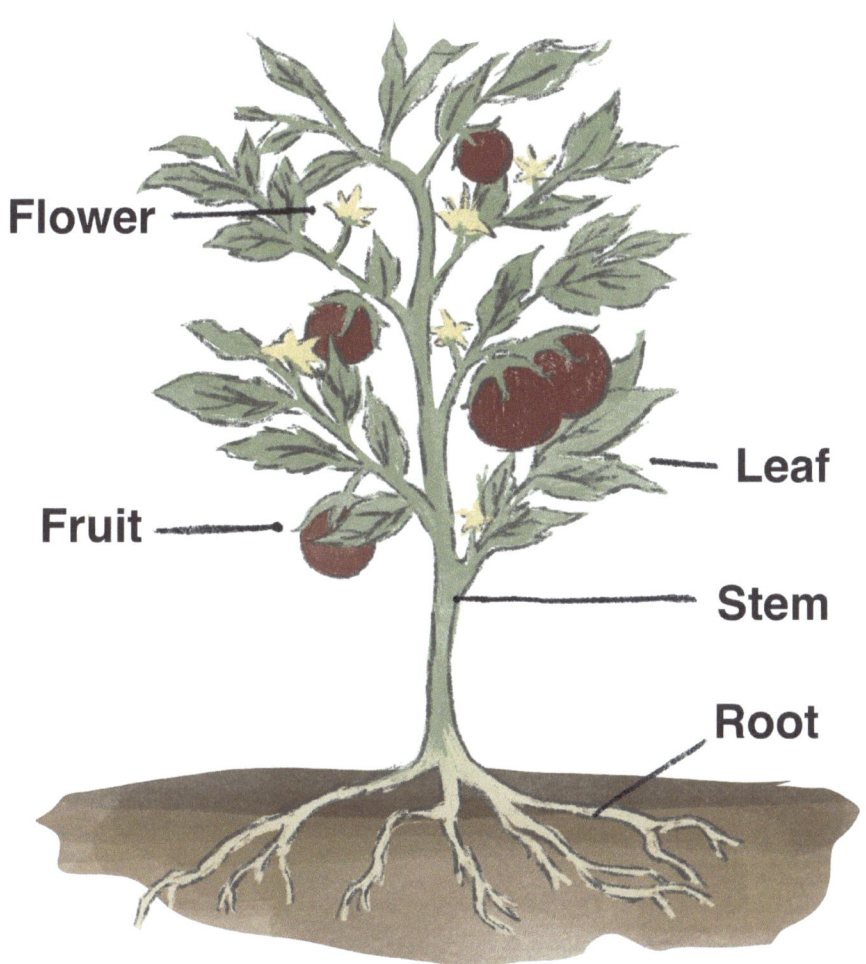

Parts of a Plant:

1. **Roots**: The roots are the underground part of a plant that anchor it in the soil and absorb water and nutrients. They also store food for the plant.

2. **Stems**: Stems are the above-ground structures of a plant that provide support and transport water, nutrients, and sugars between the roots and the rest of the plant. Stems also hold leaves, flowers, and fruits. Their primary functions are structural support, transport, and storage.

3. **Leaves**: Leaves are the main organs of photosynthesis in plants. They are usually flat and green, containing chlorophyll, which helps capture sunlight for energy conversion.
   The primary function of leaves is to produce food through photosynthesis. They also help regulate water loss through small openings called stomata.

4. **Flowers**: Flowers are the reproductive structures of flowering plants. They contain male and female reproductive organs that enable the process of pollination and subsequent seed formation. Flowers often have colorful petals to attract pollinators such as bees, butterflies, or birds. Their main function is sexual reproduction.

5. **Fruits**: Fruits develop from flowers and contain seeds. They play a crucial role in protecting and dispersing seeds. Fruits come in various shapes, sizes, and colors and can be fleshy or dry. The primary function of fruits is seed dispersal, accomplished through animals or natural forces such as wind or water.

Hands-on Activity: Plant Part Examination

Materials needed

Potted plant

Vegetables

Magnifying glass

Scissors

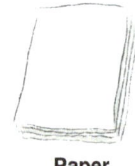
Paper

Pencil

Materials needed:
- Different plants (you can use a variety of potted plants, flowers, or vegetables)
- Magnifying glasses
- Scissors
- Paper and pencils

Examination Procedure:

1. Gather various plants with different parts (roots, stems, leaves, flowers, fruits) for examination. You can use potted plants from a garden or bring in different flowers or vegetables.

2. Set up a workspace with the plants, magnifying glasses, scissors, paper, and pencils.

3. Begin by examining the roots of a plant. Carefully remove the plant from its pot or dig out a small amount of soil to expose the roots. Observe the color, texture, and structure of the roots. Discuss their function in absorbing water and nutrients.

4. Move on to examining the stem of another plant. Look for features like the main stem, branches, and nodes or buds. Discuss the stem's function in supporting and transporting water, nutrients, and sugars.

5. Choose a plant with leaves and examine them closely. Observe the shape, color, and veining patterns of the leaves. Discuss the role of leaves in photosynthesis and their importance in producing food for the plant.

6. Select a plant with flowers and observe the different parts: petals, sepals, stamens (male reproductive organs), and pistils (female reproductive organs). Discuss the purpose of flowers in sexual reproduction and attracting pollinators.

7. Finally, examine a plant with fruits. Observe the size, shape, and color of the fruits. Discuss how fruits protect seeds and aid in their dispersal.
8. Encourage participants to sketch or take notes about each plant part they observe and discuss their findings as a group.

This hands-on activity will allow participants to actively engage with different plant parts, fostering a deeper understanding of their functions and importance in plant life.

Week 3: Soil and Composting

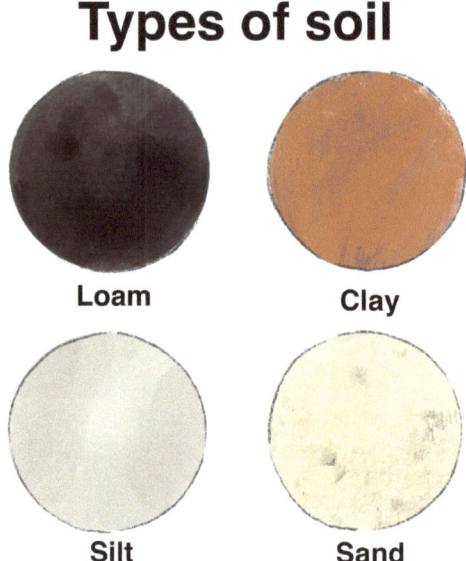

Objectives:
- Explore the importance of soil in gardening.
- Discuss the different types of soil and their characteristics.
- Learn about composting and its benefits to the garden ecosystem.

Soil plays a crucial role in gardening because it provides a foundation for plants to grow and thrive. It is a home for plant roots, supplies essential nutrients, and helps retain moisture. Let's explore the importance of soil in gardening in more detail.

Types of Soil
Different types of soil have distinct characteristics that affect plant growth. Here are some common types of soil:

1. **Sandy soil**: Sandy soil has larger particles and feels gritty. It drains water quickly, which can be good for some plants but doesn't retain moisture well. Sandy soil is often low in nutrients, so gardeners may need to add compost or fertilizer to improve its fertility.

2. **Clay soil**: Clay soil has very fine particles and feels sticky when wet. It retains water and nutrients better than sandy soil but can become compacted and drain poorly. Gardeners can improve clay soil by adding organic matter like compost or peat moss to increase drainage and loosen it up.

3. **Loam soil**: Loam soil is a cross between sandy and clay soils. It has a good mixture of particle sizes, allowing it to retain moisture while draining well. Generally, loam soil is ideal for gardening because it is fertile and provides a good structure for plant roots to grow.

4. **Silt soil:** Silt soil has medium-sized particles and feels smooth. It retains moisture well and is more fertile than sandy soil. However, it is prone to compaction and may require amendments like compost to improve its structure.

Benefits of Composting

Composting is a process that turns organic waste into nutrient-rich soil amendment called compost. Composting is beneficial to the garden ecosystem in several ways:

1. **Improves soil fertility**: Compost is rich in nutrients plants need for healthy growth. When added to the soil, it enhances the soil's fertility and provides a steady supply of essential elements.

2. **Enhances soil structure**: Compost improves the structure of soil, especially heavy clay or sandy soils. It helps clay soil drain better and increases moisture retention in sandy soil, creating a more balanced environment for plants.

3. **Increases microbial activity**: Compost contains beneficial microorganisms that contribute to a healthy soil ecosystem. These microbes break down organic matter, release nutrients, and suppress harmful pathogens.

4. **Reduces waste**: Composting allows you to recycle kitchen scraps, yard waste, and other organic materials that would otherwise end up in landfills. It's an environmentally friendly way to reduce waste and promote sustainability.

Getting Started with Composting

To start composting, you can collect fruit and vegetable scraps, coffee grounds, yard trimmings, and leaves. These materials decompose over time, creating nutrient-rich compost. You can add the compost to your garden beds or use it as a top dressing for existing plants.

Remember, soil and composting are important aspects of gardening. By understanding different soil types and composting techniques, you can create a healthier and more productive garden ecosystem.

Week 4: Seeds and Germination

Objectives:
- Learn about the life cycle of a plant from seed to maturity.
- Explore different types of seeds (vegetable, fruit, flower) and their germination requirements.
- Conduct a seed germination experiment and observe the growth process.

Let's explore the life cycle of a plant from seed to maturity and learn about different types of seeds and their germination requirements. We can also conduct a simple seed germination experiment to observe the growth process.

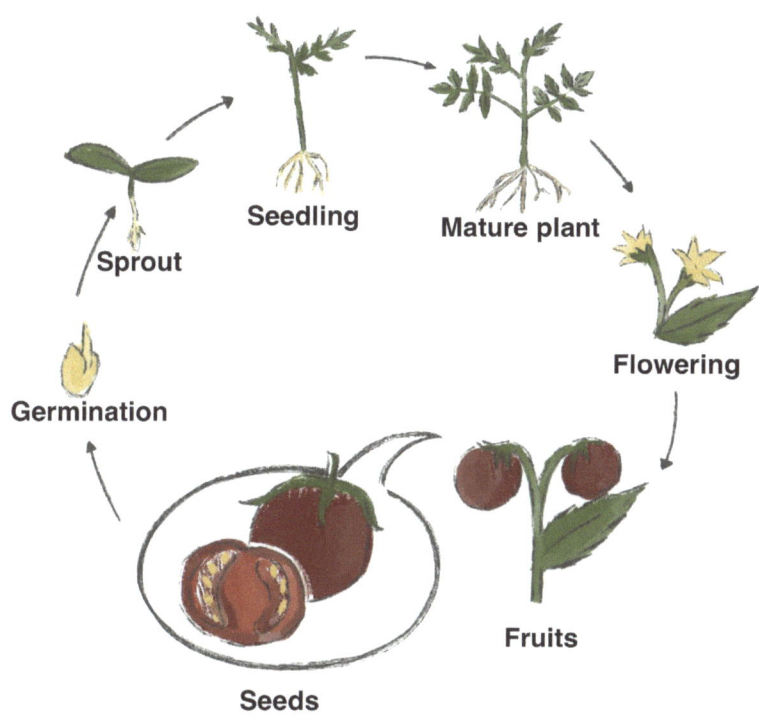

Life Cycle of a Plant:

1. **Seed**: A plant's life cycle begins with a seed. Seeds are formed when a flower is pollinated. They contain the embryo of a new plant along with a food source to support its early growth.

2. **Germination**: Germination is the process by which a seed begins to grow into a new plant. For germination to occur, seeds require certain conditions: water, warmth, and oxygen. The seed absorbs water, which activates the embryo. The warmth and oxygen

help the embryo break through the seed coat.
3. **Seedling**: After germination, the seed develops into a seedling. It grows roots downward into the soil to absorb water and nutrients. Meanwhile, the shoot emerges above the ground, developing leaves to harness sunlight for photosynthesis.

4. **Growth**: As the seedling continues to grow, it develops more leaves, stems, and roots. It uses photosynthesis to convert sunlight, water, and carbon dioxide into energy and nutrients.

5. **Reproduction**: Once the plant has matured, it produces flowers or cones, depending on the type of plant. These flowers contain reproductive structures that insects, wind, or other methods can pollinate.

6. **Seed Production**: If the flowers are successfully pollinated, they will produce seeds. The seeds contain the genetic information necessary to create new plants, continuing the life cycle.

Types of Seeds and Germination Requirements:

- **Vegetable Seeds**: Vegetable seeds include seeds from plants like tomatoes, lettuce, carrots, and peppers. These seeds require suitable soil, moisture, and appropriate temperatures for germination. Each vegetable seed may have specific temperature and moisture requirements for successful germination.

- **Fruit Seeds**: Fruit seeds come from plants like apples, oranges, watermelons, and strawberries. Fruit seeds often require a moist environment, warmth, and sometimes light for germination. Some fruit seeds may also need to go through a process called stratification, which involves exposing them to cold temperatures to break their dormancy.

- **Flower Seeds**: Flower seeds come from plants like sunflowers, roses, marigolds, and tulips. The germination requirements for flower seeds can vary depending on the specific type of flower. Some flower seeds need light for germination, while others require darkness. They may also have different temperature and moisture requirements.

Seed Germination Experiment:

Here's a simple seed germination experiment you can conduct:

Materials needed:

- Different types of seeds (vegetable, fruit, and flower)
- Small pots or containers
- Potting soil
- Water
- Labels or markers
- Plastic wrap or a clear plastic bag
- Sunlight or a grow light

Procedure:
1. Fill the pots or containers with potting soil.
2. Plant a few seeds of each type (vegetable, fruit, and flower) in separate pots. Follow the instructions on the seed packet for proper planting depth.
3. Water the pots thoroughly to ensure the soil is moist.
4. Label each pot with the type of seed planted.
5. Cover each pot with plastic wrap or place it inside a clear plastic bag to create a mini greenhouse effect that retains moisture.
6. Place the pots in a sunny location or under a grow light.
7. Check the pots daily and water them as needed to keep the soil moist but not overly wet.
8. Observe the pots over a period of days or weeks, noting any changes or growth you observe.
9. Record your observations and compare the seeds' germination and growth processes.

Week 5: Planting and Transplanting

Objectives:
- Discuss the proper techniques for planting seeds and seedlings.
- Learn about spacing, watering, and sunlight requirements for different plants.
- Conduct a planting activity in the school garden or individual pots.

Planting seeds and seedlings is an exciting activity that allows us to grow new plants. Here are some proper techniques for planting seeds and seedlings at a 5th-grade level.

How to Plant Seeds and Seedlings

1. **Gather the necessary materials**: Before you start planting, make sure you have the right materials, such as seeds or seedlings, soil, pots or a garden bed, water, and gardening tools like a trowel or a small shovel.

2. **Choose the right location**: Find a suitable location for your plants. Most plants require sunlight to grow, so look for an area that receives at least 6 hours of direct sunlight each day. If you're planting indoors, place the pots near a sunny window or use grow lights.

3. **Prepare the soil**: Good soil is essential for the growth of plants. Loosen the soil using a trowel or shovel, removing any rocks, weeds, or debris. Add organic matter like compost to enrich the soil and improve its fertility.

4. **Planting seeds**: Follow the instructions on the seed packet to determine the planting depth and spacing for the specific type of seed you have. Dig a small hole in the soil using your finger or a trowel, place the seed in the hole, and cover it with the soil. Gently pat the soil down to ensure good contact between the seed and the soil.

5. **Planting seedlings**: If you're using seedlings, carefully remove them from their containers, being mindful not to damage the roots. Dig a hole in the soil slightly larger than the seedling's root ball. Place the seedling in the hole, ensuring the top of the root ball is level with the soil surface. Fill the hole with soil and lightly press it down.

6. **Spacing**: Proper spacing is important for each plant to receive adequate sunlight, water, and nutrients. Follow the instructions on the seed packet or do some research to determine the recommended spacing between plants.

7. **Watering**: Watering is crucial for the growth of plants. After planting, gently water the seeds or seedlings using a watering can or a hose with a gentle spray nozzle. Be careful not to overwater, as excessive moisture can lead to root rot. Check the soil regularly and water when it feels dry to the touch.

8. **Sunlight requirements**: Different plants have unique sunlight requirements. Some plants prefer full sun, while others prefer partial shade. Research the specific needs of the plants you are growing to ensure they receive the right amount of sunlight.

9. **Take care of your plants**: Once you plant your seeds or seedlings, it's important to continue caring for them. Plant care often includes regular watering, removing weeds, and protecting them from pests if necessary. Pay attention to any specific care instructions for the plants you are growing.

Conducting a planting activity in the school garden or individual pots is a great way to put these techniques into practice. Follow the steps above and involve your classmates or fellow students in the process. Make observations, record data, and document the progress of your plants as they grow. Remember to have fun and enjoy the experience of watching your plants thrive!

Week 6: Garden Maintenance

Objectives:
- Discuss the importance of regular garden maintenance.
- Learn about weeding, watering, and pest control methods.
- Assign students specific tasks to help maintain the school garden.

Regular maintenance is essential to keep our school garden healthy and beautiful. It involves handling different tasks like weeding, watering, and pest control. Let's learn about each of these tasks and why they are important.

1. **Weeding**: Weeds are unwanted plants that can compete with garden plants for sunlight, water, and nutrients. You'll need to remove weeds regularly to prevent them from taking over the garden. Weeding helps the plants we want to grow healthy and strong.

2. **Watering**: Plants need water to survive and grow. Regular watering is necessary, especially during dry periods, to keep the soil moist and provide enough water to the plants' roots. Water the plants gently and at the base to avoid damaging their leaves.

3. **Pest control**: Pests like insects and animals can harm the plants in our garden. Some pests eat the leaves or fruits, while others may spread diseases. Keep an eye out for pests and take measures to control them. This can include using natural remedies or environmentally friendly pest control methods to protect the plants.

Team-Based Garden Maintenance

To maintain our school garden, we can assign specific tasks to different students. Here are some tasks that students can help with:

1. **Weeding team**: A group of students can be responsible for regularly checking the garden for weeds and carefully removing them. They can use gloves and small gardening tools like trowels to remove the weeds from the roots.

2. **Watering team**: Another group of students can take turns watering the garden. They can use watering cans or hoses with a gentle spray nozzle to water the plants at their base. It's crucial to ensure that each plant receives enough water without overwatering them.

3. **Pest control team**: A team of students can learn about different pests and their control methods. They can monitor the garden for signs of pest infestations and take appropriate action. This can include using organic insecticides, introducing beneficial insects, or employing physical barriers like netting or fences to protect the plants.

4. **Plant care team**: Students can be assigned specific tasks related to monitoring the overall health of the plants in the garden. They can check for signs of diseases, nutrient deficiencies, or any other issues. They can then report their findings to the teacher or garden coordinator, who can take further steps to address the problems.

5. **Harvesting team**: When the plants are ready for harvest, a group of students can be in

charge of harvesting the fruits, vegetables, or herbs. They can ensure that the produce is picked at the right time and handled carefully.

6. **Composting team**: Students can learn about the importance of composting and manage a compost pile or bin in the garden. They can collect plant trimmings, fallen leaves, and other organic matter and turn it into nutrient-rich compost for the garden.

By assigning specific tasks to students, not only do we ensure that the garden is well-maintained, but we also provide valuable learning opportunities. Students can learn about plant care, teamwork, problem-solving, and the importance of environmental stewardship.

In conclusion, regular garden maintenance is crucial for the health and beauty of the school garden. Weeding, watering, and pest control are key tasks that require consistent attention. By assigning specific tasks to students, we can engage them in the process and foster a sense of responsibility towards the garden. Through this hands-on experience, students can learn important skills and develop a deeper appreciation for nature and the environment.

Week 7: Harvesting Fruits, Vegetables, and Herbs

Harvesting fruits, vegetables, and herbs is an exciting and rewarding process. Let's explore the steps involved in harvesting garden produce at a 5th-grade level:

1. **Determining the right time**: Different fruits, vegetables, and herbs have specific signs that indicate they are ready for harvest. For example, ripe fruits usually change color and become slightly soft. Vegetables are generally harvested when they are firm and have reached a suitable size. Herbs can be harvested once they have grown enough leaves and have a strong aroma.

2. **Gathering the necessary tools**: Before starting the harvest, gather the tools you'll need, such as gardening gloves, a small knife or scissors, a basket or bucket to collect the produce, and a clean towel or cloth.

3. **Handling the produce with care**: When harvesting, it's important to handle the fruits, vegetables, and herbs gently to avoid bruising or damaging them. Doing so helps to maintain their quality and flavor.

4. **Cutting or picking**: For fruits like apples or pears, you can use a small knife to cut the stem near the fruit. For vegetables like tomatoes or cucumbers, you can twist or gently

pull the stems off the plant. You can harvest herbs by cutting the stems just above a leaf node, where leaves emerge from the stem.

5. **Storing the harvest**: After harvesting, it's crucial to store the produce properly to keep it fresh. Fruits and vegetables can be stored in a cool, dry place or refrigerated if needed. Herbs can be air-dried by hanging them upside down in a well-ventilated area. They can also be frozen or preserved by making herb-infused oils or drying them using a dehydrator.

Using and Preserving Garden Produce

Once you've harvested your garden produce, there are several ways to use and preserve them:

- **Cooking and eating fresh**: The most immediate way to enjoy your harvest is to incorporate it into your meals. You can add freshly harvested vegetables to salads, stir-fries, or sandwiches. Herbs can be used to enhance the flavors of various dishes. Fruits can be eaten as they are or used in recipes like fruit salads or smoothies.

- **Freezing**: Freezing is a popular method of preserving fruits and vegetables. Before freezing, they are blanched to preserve their color, flavor, and texture. The process involves quickly boiling and then cooling the produce in ice water. Once blanched, the produce is packed in airtight containers or freezer bags and stored in the freezer for later use.

- **Canning**: Canning is a method used to preserve fruits, vegetables, and even jams and jellies. It involves heating the produce in jars or cans with a specific sugar or acid solution to kill bacteria and prevent spoilage. The sealed jars can be stored in a cool, dark place and enjoyed throughout the year.

- **Drying**: Drying is a traditional method of preserving herbs, fruits, and certain vegetables. You can air-dry herbs by hanging them upside down or using a dehydrator to remove the moisture. Fruits and vegetables can be dried by slicing them into thin pieces and placing them in a dehydrator or an oven at a low temperature until they are dry and crisp."

Herb Salad Dressing Recipe

Here's an easy recipe for a flavorful herb-infused salad dressing:

Ingredients:

- 1/2 cup extra-virgin olive oil
- 1/4 cup vinegar (such as balsamic or apple cider vinegar)
- 1 teaspoon Dijon mustard
- 1 garlic clove, minced
- 1 tablespoon fresh lemon juice
- 1 tablespoon chopped fresh herbs (such as basil, parsley, or dill)
- Salt and pepper to taste

Instructions:

1. Whisk the olive oil, vinegar, Dijon mustard, minced garlic, and lemon juice in a small bowl until well combined.

2. Add the chopped fresh herbs to the dressing and stir to combine.

3. Season with salt and pepper to taste, adjusting the amount according to your preference.

4. Let the dressing sit for at least 10 minutes to allow the flavors to meld together.

5. Give the dressing a final whisk before serving over your favorite salad greens or vegetables.

Note: You can store any leftover dressing in an airtight container in the refrigerator for up to one week. Just give it a good shake before using it again. Enjoy!

Week 8: Common Garden Pests and Their Impact on Plants

Objectives:
- Explore common garden pests and their impact on plants.
- Discuss organic methods of pest control.
- Learn about beneficial insects and their role in maintaining a healthy garden ecosystem.

In a garden, various pests can cause damage to plants. Here are some common garden pests and the impact they can have on plants:

- **Aphids**: Aphids are small, soft-bodied insects that suck sap from plant stems and leaves. They can cause wilting, stunted growth, and distorted foliage. Additionally, aphids excrete a sticky substance called honeydew, which can attract ants and promote the growth of sooty mold.

- **Slugs and Snails**: Slugs and snails are mollusks that feed on plant leaves, stems, and fruits. They leave behind irregular holes and trails of slime. These pests are more active in damp and cool conditions.

- **Caterpillars**: Caterpillars are the larval stage of butterflies and moths. They feed on leaves, causing visible damage such as chewed foliage. Some caterpillars are more destructive than others, but they can defoliate plants if present in large numbers.

- **Whiteflies**: Whiteflies are tiny, winged insects that feed on plant sap. They can cause yellowing, wilting, and premature leaf drop. Additionally, whiteflies excrete honeydew, which can attract ants and promote the growth of sooty mold.

- **Beetles**: Various beetles, such as Colorado potato beetles and Japanese beetles, can damage garden plants. They chew on leaves, flowers, and fruits, leading to skeletonized foliage and reduced crop yield.

Organic Methods of Pest Control

Instead of relying on chemical pesticides, organic methods of pest control focus on natural and environmentally friendly techniques to manage garden pests. Here are some organic methods you can use:

1. **Handpicking**: Inspect plants regularly and manually remove pests like slugs, snails, caterpillars, and beetles from your garden. Drop them into a bucket of soapy water to prevent them from returning.

2. **Beneficial Insects**: Encourage beneficial insects like ladybugs, lacewings, and praying mantises to your garden. These insects feed on garden pests and help control their population naturally. You can attract them by planting flowers that provide nectar and pollen.

3. **Companion Planting**: Some plants have natural pest-repellent properties. For example, marigolds can deter aphids and nematodes, while garlic and onions can repel various insects. By interplanting these companion plants with vulnerable crops, you can reduce pest problems.

4. **Natural Barriers**: Create physical barriers to keep pests away from your plants. For example, you can use floating row covers to protect plants from flying insects or erect fences to deter larger pests like rabbits and deer.

5. **Organic Sprays:** You can make organic sprays using ingredients like neem oil, garlic, or soap to control pests. These sprays are effective against aphids, mites, and other soft-bodied insects and may be less harmful to beneficial insects.

Beneficial Insects and Their Role in Garden Ecosystems

Beneficial insects are crucial in maintaining a healthy garden ecosystem. They control pest populations and promote pollination. Here are some examples of beneficial insects and their roles:

- **Ladybugs**: Ladybugs, also known as lady beetles, feed on aphids, mealybugs, mites, and other soft-bodied insects. They are excellent natural predators and can help control pest populations in your garden.

- **Lacewings**: Lacewings are delicate insects with transparent wings. Both adult lacewings and their larvae are voracious predators, feeding on aphids, mites, thrips, and other small insects.

- **Praying Mantises**: Praying mantises are ambush predators that feed on many insects, including beetles, moths, flies, and grasshoppers. They are highly skilled hunters and can help control pest populations in the garden.

- **Hoverflies**: Hoverflies, also known as flower flies, are excellent pollinators. They resemble bees or wasps but do not sting. Hoverfly larvae are predators and feed on aphids, thrips, and other soft-bodied insects.

- **Bees**: Bees are perhaps the most well-known beneficial insects due to their vital role in pollination. Bees visit flowers to collect nectar and pollen, transferring pollen grains from one flower to another, which allows plants to produce fruits and seeds. Without bees, many plants would struggle to reproduce.

- **Parasitic Wasps:** Parasitic wasps are small, non-stinging wasps that lay their eggs inside or on other insects. The wasp larvae then develop by feeding on the host insects, eventually killing them. Parasitic wasps are particularly effective at controlling caterpillars, aphids, and other pests.

- **Ground Beetles**: Ground beetles are nocturnal predators that feed on slugs, snails, caterpillars, and other insects. They are beneficial in controlling pest populations, especially those that reside on the ground.

These are just a few examples of beneficial insects and their roles in the garden ecosystem. By attracting and supporting these beneficial insects, gardeners can reduce the need for harmful pesticides and create a more balanced and sustainable environment for their plants.

Week 9: Garden Design Basics

Objectives
- Discuss the basics of garden design and planning.
- Explore different garden layouts and their purposes.
- Assign students the task of designing their own garden layout.

Garden design and planning can be a fun and creative process. It involves thinking about the layout of plants, flowers, and other elements to create a beautiful and functional outdoor space. Here are some basics of garden design that you can explore at a 5th-grade level:

Assessing the Space: It's essential to understand the available space before designing a garden. Consider the area's size, shape, and features, such as:
- Sunlight
- Soil type
- Drainage

These factors will help determine what types of plants will thrive in the garden.

1. **Garden Layout**: There are several garden layouts to consider, each with its own purpose. Here are a few of the most common:

    a. **Rectangular Beds**: This layout involves organizing plants and flowers in rectangular beds, creating a structured and organized look. It's suitable for formal gardens or areas with limited space.

    b. **Circular Gardens**: Circular gardens have a central focal point, such as a tree or a fountain, and plants arranged in circular patterns around it. They create a sense of harmony and can be visually appealing.

    c. **Pathway Gardens**: These gardens have pathways that lead visitors through the garden, allowing them to enjoy the different plants and features. Pathways can be made of stone, gravel, or other materials.

    d. **Raised Bed Gardens**: Raised beds are elevated from the ground and are helpful for growing plants in areas with poor soil quality. You can make them out of wood, bricks, or other materials.

2. **Plant Selection**: Once you have decided on a garden layout, it's time to choose the plants. Consider the climate, soil type, and sunlight conditions in your area. Select plants that will thrive in these conditions and complement each other in terms of color, texture, and height.

3. **Creating Zones**: You can divide your garden into different zones based on the plants' needs and purposes. For example, you might have a flower zone, a vegetable zone, and a relaxation zone with seating and shade.

4. **Maintenance**: A well-designed garden should be easy to maintain. Consider the time and effort required for watering, weeding, and pruning when planning your garden layout. It's helpful to choose plants that are suitable for your available time and resources.

Assigning the task of designing a garden layout to students can be a great hands-on project. Provide them with graph paper or a blank sheet of paper and encourage them to draw their ideal garden design. They can research different plants and their requirements and include those in their layout. Encourage creativity and allow them to express their ideas freely.

You can also discuss the importance of caring for the environment while designing a garden. Encourage students to consider using organic fertilizers, conserving water, and attracting beneficial insects like bees and butterflies to their gardens.

By exploring garden design and planning, students can develop their creativity, problem-solving skills, and understanding of nature.

Week 10: The Environmental Benefits of Gardening

Objectives:
- Discuss the environmental benefits of gardening.
- Explore sustainable gardening practices.
- Discuss the importance of biodiversity and its relation to gardening.

Gardening offers numerous environmental benefits and is an excellent way for individuals to contribute to sustainability efforts. Here are some key environmental benefits of gardening:

- **Carbon sequestration**: Plants play a crucial role in absorbing carbon dioxide from the atmosphere through photosynthesis. By gardening and planting trees, we can increase the overall carbon sequestration capacity, helping mitigate climate change.

- **Oxygen production**: Through photosynthesis, plants release oxygen into the atmosphere, which is vital for all living organisms. A well-maintained garden with a diverse range of plants can significantly increase oxygen levels in the surrounding environment.

- **Water filtration**: Gardens with healthy soil act as natural filters, preventing pollutants from reaching water sources. The roots of plants help to stabilize the soil, reducing erosion and the runoff of harmful substances into nearby streams, rivers, and lakes.

- **Urban heat island effect mitigation**: Urban areas often suffer from the urban heat island effect, where concrete and asphalt absorb and radiate heat, leading to higher temperatures. By incorporating green spaces and gardens, particularly with trees, we can mitigate this effect by providing shade, cooling the surrounding air, and reducing energy consumption.
- **Wildlife habitat creation**: Gardens, especially those with diverse plant species, can attract and support a wide array of wildlife. Birds, bees, butterflies, and other beneficial insects are attracted to flowering plants, providing them with food and shelter. This creates a balanced ecosystem and contributes to biodiversity.

Sustainable Gardening Practices

Sustainable gardening practices further enhance the environmental benefits and minimize negative impacts. These practices include:

- **Organic gardening**: Avoiding synthetic fertilizers and pesticides helps protect soil health, water quality, and the overall ecosystem. Instead, organic gardeners use natural alternatives such as compost, mulch, and biological pest control methods.

- **Water conservation**: Efficient water use is crucial in gardening. Practices like mulching, drip irrigation, and rainwater harvesting can significantly reduce water waste. Choosing native and drought-tolerant plants also helps conserve water resources.

- **Composting and recycling**: Composting organic waste, such as kitchen scraps and garden trimmings, reduces landfill waste while providing nutrient-rich soil amendments. Additionally, recycling garden materials like containers and utilizing recycled materials for hardscaping minimizes environmental impact.

Gardening Supports Biodiversity

Biodiversity plays a vital role in maintaining healthy ecosystems, and gardening can support biodiversity in several ways:

- **Plant diversity**: Incorporating a variety of plant species in a garden attracts different pollinators and beneficial insects. Native plants are particularly valuable as they provide food and shelter for local wildlife and contribute to the preservation of regional biodiversity.

- **Food sources for wildlife**: Planting flowers, fruits, and seeds that provide nectar, pollen, and berries supports pollinators, birds, and other wildlife. This creates a food web within the garden and promotes a balanced ecosystem.

- **Habitat creation**: Gardens with diverse plantings, including trees, shrubs, and groundcovers, offer habitats for a range of organisms. Birds can build nests, insects can find shelter, and small mammals can establish homes, contributing to the overall biodiversity of the area.

- **Genetic diversity**: By growing a wide variety of plant species and avoiding monocultures, gardeners help preserve genetic diversity. This is important for the resilience and adaptability of plants in the face of environmental challenges like pests, diseases, and climate change.

In summary, gardening provides numerous environmental benefits, including carbon sequestration, oxygen production, water filtration, urban heat island mitigation, and wildlife habitat creation. By adopting sustainable gardening practices and promoting biodiversity, individuals can positively impact the environment and contribute to a healthier, more sustainable planet.

Throughout the curriculum, it is essential to incorporate hands-on activities, field trips to local gardens or farms, and opportunities for students to care for and observe plants firsthand. Additionally, consider involving students in the planning and maintenance of a school garden, if available, to provide a practical and engaging learning experience.

www.ingramcontent.com/pod-product-compliance
Lightning Source LLC
LaVergne TN
LVHW071700060526
838201LV00037B/393